FOOD & HOW TO COOK IT!

FRUIT AND VEGETABLES

BY CLAIRE LLEWELLYN

WITH RECIPES BY CLARE O'SHEA

WAYLAND

First published in 2009 by Wayland
Copyright © Wayland 2009

Wayland
338 Euston Road
London NW1 3BH

Wayland Australia
Level 17/207 Kent Street
Sydney NSW 2000

Commissioning editor: Jennifer Sanderson
Designer: www.rawshock.co.uk
Photographer: Andy Crawford
Illustrator: Ian Thompson
Hand model: Camilla Lloyd
Proofreader and indexer: Susie Brooks
Consultant: Clare O'Shea – Clare has taught food
technology for more than 17 years in various London-based
schools. She is currently Head of Food Technology
at London Academy, where she teaches years 7 to 13.
The Academy delivers GCSE Hospitality and Catering to
years 10 and 11, A Level Food Technology and the Food
Hygiene Certificate.

British Cataloguing in Publication Data
  O'Shea, Clare.
  Fruit & vegetables. -- (Food and how to cook it)
  1. Fruit in human nutrition--
  Juvenile literature.
  2. Vegetables in human nutrition--Juvenile literature.
  3. Cookery (Fruit)--Juvenile literature.
  4. Cookery (Vegetables)--Juvenile literature.
  I. Title II. Series III. Llewellyn, Claire.
  641.3'4-dc22

ISBN: 978 0 7502 5659 9

Printed in China

Wayland is a division of Hachette Children's Books,
an Hachette UK company.
www.hachette.co.uk

Picture Acknowledgements:
All photography by Andy Crawford, except Tomas del Amo/
Alamy: 10; Dorling Kindersley/Getty Images: 19T; Frank
Herholdt/Getty Images: 43; Gary Holscher/AgStock Images/
Corbis: 31; iStockphoto: 6, 23T; Ron Levine/Getty Images: 4;
Andrew Linscott/Alamy: 39; Stuart O'Sullivan/Getty Images: 35;
Thomas Weightman/Alamy: 15;

Note:
In preparation of this book, all due care has been exercised with
regard to the advice, activities and techniques depicted. The publishers
regret that they can accept no liability for any loss or injury sustained.
Always follow manufacturers' advice when using kitchen appliances
and kitchen equipment.

The website addresses (URLs) included in this book were valid at the
time of going to press. However, because of the nature of the Internet,
it is possible that some addresses may have changed, or sites may have
changed or closed down since publication. While the authors and
publishers regret any inconvenience this may cause the readers, no
responsibility for any such changes can be accepted by either the
authors or the publishers.

Contents

Plants and a balanced diet

Fruit and vegetables are the edible parts of plants. There is an enormous variety of fruit, from apples and plums to marrows and peppers. Vegetables include carrots, cauliflower, onions and potatoes.

Growing fruit and vegetables

Most of the fruit and vegetables that people buy in supermarkets are grown on farms and market gardens. Some farmers grow organic produce that has not been sprayed with pesticides and has been grown using only natural fertilisers. Many varieties of both fruit and vegetables are grown locally, according to the season, while others are imported from warmer countries. Some people grow their own fruit and vegetables in their garden.

A vegetarian diet

Many people choose not to eat meat or fish. Instead they rely on dairy foods and plants, such as legumes, for their protein. A vegetarian diet is a healthy choice so long as it includes plenty of pulses, nuts and seeds. These foods contain proteins but, unlike the proteins in meat or fish, they must be combined with one another to provide a complete form of protein. For example, baked beans on toast provide complete protein because they combine haricot beans (a pulse) with wheat (a seed grain).

A healthy diet

The food we eat, or our diet, is an important part of a healthy lifestyle. There are five main food groups that contain different nutrients that work together to keep the body healthy. These groups are often shown on a 'food plate', where you can see the proportions in which they should be eaten (see page 5).

Added to these food groups is water. We need about six to eight glasses of water each day to keep our bodies healthy.

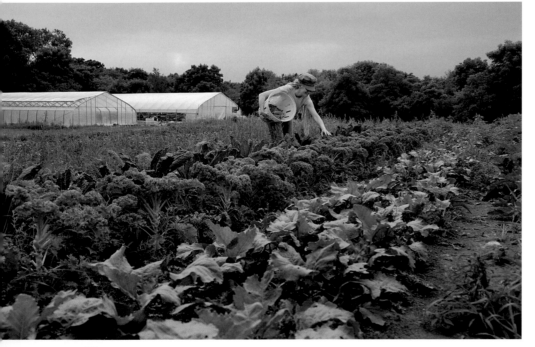

This farm worker is harvesting a field of organic kale. Organic produce is grown without the use of pesticides and artificial fertilisers.

The food plate

Fruit and vegetables: Full of vitamins and minerals, these foods protect our body and reduce the risk of heart disease, stroke and some cancers. The fibre in them helps to bulk up our food and keep our digestive system healthy. Fruit and vegetables are low in fat so they fill us up without unnecessary calories.

Carbohydrates: These provide us with energy. Starchy carbohydrates, which include grains and cereals, should make up about 30 per cent of the food we eat. Starchy carbohydrates are an important source of energy for sportsmen and women because they release the energy slowly, keeping them going for longer.

FRUIT AND VEGETABLES

CARBOHYDRATES

PROTEIN

FATS

MILK AND DAIRY

Protein: This builds and repairs our bones, muscles, skin, hair and body tissues. Meat, fish, eggs and pulses, which provide body-building proteins, should make up about 15 per cent of our total daily diet.

Fats: These keep us warm and can also be stored in the body for energy. Foods that are high in saturated fats (fats from animal sources) or sugar, such as cakes, biscuits and crisps, should be eaten only in small amounts (about 8 per cent of our total diet). Fats found in oily fish, olives and nuts and seeds are called unsaturated fats. Saturated fats are linked to an increased risk of heart disease. Eating unsaturated fats is a healthier alternative.

Dairy: Dairy products include milk, butter, yoghurt and cheese. They are packed with nutrients, such as calcium, magnesium, Vitamin K, zinc and protein, and help to build strong bones and teeth. Yoghurt is full of good bacteria and improves our immune system and digestive health. It is best to eat cheese in moderation because it is high in fat.

FOOD FACTS

Doctors advise us to eat at least five portions of fruit and vegetables each day. For example, one portion is:
7 cherry tomatoes
5-centimetre piece of cucumber

Half a red pepper
3 heaped tablespoons of cooked vegetables
1 apple
1 orange
150ml fresh fruit juice

Looking at vegetables

From savoury onions to sweet roasted parsnips, vegetables add goodness and flavour to our diet. Once served only as an accompaniment, they are now used to make meals in their own right, satisfying vegetarians and meat-eaters alike.

Eating vegetables

There are so many kinds of vegetable available that they provide a huge variety of vitamins and minerals. They can be eaten raw in salads or cooked in soups, stuffed or baked as a meal in themselves, or added to stews, risottos, pasta and pizza. They also make tasty side dishes to main courses.

The nutrients in vegetables are easily destroyed by cooking, so you should try to eat some of them raw. If you are boiling them, cook for them for as short a time as possible in very little liquid. This is called blanching. Vegetables can also be steamed, roasted, fried, barbequed, grilled or stir-fried.

Processing vegetables

After harvesting, vegetables may be frozen, dried, canned, made into sauces or added to all kinds of ready meals, such as soups and broths. Fresh vegetables can be preserved by boiling them with vinegar, sugar, spices and fruit. This produces tasty pickles and chutneys and other kinds of relish.

Processing vegetables allows us to eat them all year round, even when they are out of season. For example, tinned tomatoes are useful in the winter, when fresh tomatoes have less flavour.

 Fresh peas are very tender but quickly turn hard and starchy. If they are frozen within hours of picking, they stay soft and sweet.

 FOOD FACTS

Many plants are grown for their seeds, which are dried in order to preserve them. They are known as pulses and include lentils, chickpeas, kidney beans, haricot beans and butter beans.

Vegetable types

Vegetable fruits: These fleshy, seed-bearing fruits are classed as vegetables because they taste less sweet than other fruits. They include aubergine, courgette, peppers, squashes, cucumbers and tomatoes.

Leaves: These are the edible leaves of a plant and include cabbage, lettuce, spinach and pak choi.

Flowers: These are the edible flowers of a plant, for example cauliflower and broccoli.

Fungi: Edible fungi are known as mushrooms. There are many varieties, including oyster, shiitake, chestnut and button.

Bulbs: These are layered, segmented vegetables that grow just below the surface of the ground and produce leafy shoots. They include onions, shallots, garlic, spring onions and leeks.

Tubers: These are vegetables that grow under the ground on the root of a plant. They include potatoes, sweet potatoes, yams and Jerusalem artichokes.

Roots: These are the swollen root of a plant and include carrots, turnips, beetroot, swedes, radishes, parsnips and celeriacs.

Seeds: The seeds and sometimes the pods of plants such as broad beans, French beans, runner beans and peas are eaten.

Stems: These are the stalks of a plant. They include asparagus, celery and kohlrabi.

Looking at fruits

For many people, sweet fruit is irresistible and includes some of the best-tasting foods that nature can provide. From crunchy green apples to soft white peaches, fruit provides us with fabulous flavours, which cannot be replaced by any other foods.

Eating fruit

Most fruits, such as apples, bananas, satsumas and grapes, are good for snacking and can be eaten raw. Alternatively, they can be sliced over breakfast cereals or added to salads. Fruit is used in dozens of desserts, including tarts, pies, crumbles, flans, jellies, ice creams, sorbets, mousses and trifles. It can also be squeezed or blended to make juices, smoothies and other drinks. Some fruits are traditionally served with meat; think of roast pork with apple sauce, gammon and pineapple, and roast turkey with cranberry sauce. The fruit contrasts with the richness of the meat and helps our body to digest it. Many fruits, such as berries and tropical fruits, make the perfect end to a meal. It is healthiest to eat them as they are, without fatty creams and custards.

In summer, when fruits are plentiful, they can be boiled up with sugar to make jam. In winter, bitter oranges can be made into marmalade.

Dried apricots make a delicious and nutritious snack – in fact, they have a far greater nutritional value than fresh apricots because their content is so concentrated. They contain fibre, vitamins and minerals, such as iron.

Processing fruit

Fruit is delicious when it is fresh, but it can also be preserved. Dried fruit, such as raisins, sultanas, currants, prunes and apricots, can be added to muesli or used in scones, tea loaves and cakes. Dried fruit can also be soaked in water and cooked until it is soft. Fruit can be canned, frozen, preserved in jams and marmalades, bottled in syrup, or made into sauces. Frozen fruit retains more of its nutrients than tinned fruit.

Fruit groups

Tropical fruits: This diverse group includes fruits that grow in the warmest parts of the world. Bananas, mangoes, pineapples, papayas, passion fruit and kiwi fruit are all tropical fruits.

Orchard fruits: These grow on fruit trees on farms and in market gardens. They include apples, pears, plums, cherries, apricots and peaches.

Citrus fruits: These are juicy fruits covered in a thick peel that grow on trees and shrubs in sub-tropical climates. They include oranges, lemons, limes, grapefruit and tangerines.

Berries and currants: Small, soft, juicy berries are grown on bushes or smaller plants. They include strawberries, raspberries, loganberries, blackcurrants, redcurrants and blackberries.

 FOOD FACTS

Kiwi fruit contain more Vitamin C than most citrus fruits. They also contain a lot of fibre, which helps the intestines to work properly.

Salad vegetables

Served as a starter, a side dish, or a main course, salads are colourful, delicious and nutritious. Almost any fresh vegetable can be included, according to taste and the season.

Why eat salads?

Salads are a very healthy choice because raw vegetables are bursting with goodness. Some of the vitamins and minerals that these foods contain are lost in cooking. Salad is the perfect food for a hot summer's day, although different ingredients, such as cabbage and carrots, can create tasty winter salads – a change from heavier winter meals. Salads are flexible, too. You can transform a salad into a main course by adding fish, egg or pasta. Salads are simple because many of them involve no cooking!

FOOD FACTS

Eating a side salad with each meal is an easy way to reach your five portions of fruit and vegetables a day. For maximum benefit, choose salad ingredients of different colours – green spinach, yellow and orange peppers, red tomatoes – because they contain different nutrients.

 Salads are healthy and delicious. All that chewing makes us eat more slowly, and helps us to feel 'full up'!

Salads around the world

There are dozens of salad recipes and some of them are specific to certain countries or regions. Many of these originated in hot places, where cold food is preferred during the heat of the day. *Salade niçoise,* which originated in the south of France, combines lettuce, cold potatoes, French beans, tomatoes, anchovies, hard-boiled egg and parsley. *Taboulleh*, a refreshing salad eaten throughout the Middle East, is made of bulgar wheat mixed with lots of lemon juice, mint and parsley, along with cucumber, tomato and spring onion. In a Greek salad, tangy feta cheese is combined with tomato, cucumber and olives. The world-famous *Caesar salad* includes crisp lettuce leaves served with grated cheese, crispy croutons and a garlic dressing.

Choosing and storing salad vegetables

Avoid ready-made bagged salads, which are less fresh than those prepared at home. Look for vegetables that are firm and fresh, rejecting any that are limp or soft. Store salad ingredients in the vegetable drawer in your refrigerator for up to one week.

Salad dressings

Many salads are served with a sauce, which is called a dressing. Popular salad dressings include vinaigrette, which is widely eaten throughout the world but particularly in southern Europe. In Scandinavia and Eastern Europe, dressings – for example, on potato salad – are often based on mayonnaise, yoghurt or crème fraiche and are sometimes mixed with a blue cheese for a rich, creamy dressing.

Basic vinaigrette

MAKES: 160ml	PREPARATION TIME: 5 MINUTES	COOKING TIME: NO COOKING

This dressing will work with any salad.

Ingredients
120ml extra virgin olive oil
2 tablespoons vinegar
1 teaspoon lemon juice
salt and pepper

1. Whisk all the ingredients together in a bowl.

2. Add salt and pepper to taste.

3. If not using immediately, pour the dressing into a container and shake well before using.

COOK'S TIP

You can add a teaspoon of Dijon mustard if you like.

Salade niçoise

This salad originated in the south of France. It makes a hearty main meal, perfect for a warm summer's day.

Ingredients
500g new potatoes, scrubbed
350g thin green beans, cut in half
1 small fennel bulb, thinly sliced
1 teaspoon extra virgin olive oil
lettuce leaves
12 baby plum tomatoes, cut in half
3 hard-boiled eggs, quartered
12 black olives, without stones

For the dressing
1 50g can anchovy fillets, drained
1 small garlic clove, peeled
2 teaspoons Dijon mustard
1 teaspoon lemon juice
4 teaspoons extra virgin olive oil

1. Boil water for the potatoes in a saucepan. When the water is boiling, add the potatoes and cook them for about 15 minutes, until tender. Add the beans after 10 minutes.

2. Drain the potatoes and the beans in a colander and rinse under cold running water.

3. Cut the potatoes in half and put them and the beans in a large mixing bowl. Add the fennel.

4. To make the salad dressing, put three of the anchovy fillets and the garlic into a blender. Whizz them to make a smooth purée.

5. Add the mustard, lemon juice and oil and process until smooth.

6. Pour the dressing over the vegetables in the bowl and stir well to mix.

7. Put a layer of lettuce leaves on each one of four plates. Divide the potato mixture among them.

8. Arrange the tomatoes and egg quarters around the edge of each plate. Scatter the olives over the salad.

9. Add the remaining anchovies, dividing them equally among each plate of salad. Serve immediately.

COOK'S TIP

Sprinkle some toasted pinenuts or sesame seeds over the top of the salad for extra crunch and flavour and protein.

Summer couscous salad

| SERVES: 4 | PREPARATION TIME: 20 MINUTES | COOKING TIME: NO COOKING |

This salad is a perfect accompaniment to food cooked on a barbeque.

Ingredients
250g couscous
20 cherry tomatoes, quartered
1 small red onion, peeled and finely chopped
10cm piece of cucumber, chopped
1 large carrot, peeled and grated
2 tablespoons fresh coriander, chopped
salt and pepper

For the dressing
¼ teaspoon ground cumin
1 small garlic clove, peeled and finely chopped
1 tablespoon lemon juice
3 tablespoons olive oil

1. Put the couscous into a bowl and pour over enough boiling water to cover it completely. Stir well and leave it to soak for about 15–20 minutes.

2. In the meantime, make the dressing by whisking together the cumin, garlic, lemon juice and oil in a small bowl.

3. When the couscous is ready, add the tomatoes, onion, cucumber, carrot and coriander.

4. Pour the dressing over the salad, season and mix well.

Caesar salad

| SERVES: 2–4 | PREPARATION TIME: 20 MINUTES | COOKING TIME: 10 MINUTES |

This salad is often served with a grilled breast of chicken to make chicken Caesar salad.

Ingredients
1 garlic clove, peeled and crushed
1 tablespoon olive oil
12 thin slices French bread, cut into slices
1 firm cos lettuce, torn into bite-sized pieces
1 small chicory head, sliced
4 celery sticks, sliced
30g Parmesan cheese, finely sliced

For the dressing
1 teaspoon Dijon mustard
3 tablespoons olive oil
2 teaspoons white vinegar
2 teaspoons natural yoghurt
large pinch caster sugar
½ teaspoon Worcestershire sauce
salt and pepper

1. Preheat the oven to 200°C/ gas mark 6.

2. Combine the garlic and olive oil.

3. To make croutons, brush one side of each slice of bread with the garlic oil. Bake for 10 minutes until crisp. Cut the slices into cubes.

4. Whisk together all the dressing ingredients and season to taste.

5. Put the lettuce, chicory and celery in a bowl and pour over half of the dressing. Toss the salad.

6. Divide the salad into 2 or 4 portions. Drizzle over the remaining dressing, scatter the cheese on top and add the croutons to serve.

Root vegetables and tubers sustain us during the colder seasons, when they add heartiness and sweetness to our meals and help to keep us warm. They include carrots, beetroot, parsnip, swede, celeriac, radish and different kinds of potato.

What are roots and tubers?

Most plants have thin, fibrous roots, which they use to cling to the soil and to take in water. Some plants, however, such as carrots and parsnips, use their roots in another way: to store food that will sustain the plant in the following year. The roots on these plants become fat as they swell up with sugar, starch and other carbohydrates. The roots give us energy, vitamins and minerals while being low in fat. Tubers, such as potatoes, sweet potatoes and Jerusalem artichokes, are slightly different. They are swollen pieces of stem that grow among the roots of a plant.

Where are they eaten?

Root vegetables are eaten all over the world. In many places they are staple foods. For example, in parts of Africa, a root vegetable called cassava is just as important as cereals and grains. In Russia, root vegetables are used in a salad that combines a mixture of diced, cooked vegetables, bound together with mayonnaise. In cool, temperate places, potatoes are a staple food. They are the main ingredient of famous dishes, such as the French *pommes Dauphinoise* in which layers of sliced potatoes are baked with garlic, milk and cream.

How are they eaten?

Root vegetables are good in winter dishes such as soups and stews, where they act as thickeners and add flavour. Once cooked, they are often mashed to make a soft, tasty purée. Some root vegetables can be eaten raw. For example, carrots and beetroot can be grated into salads. Potatoes are boiled, roasted, baked in their jackets or sliced and fried to make chips.

A selection of root vegetables:

1 celeriac
2 beetroot
3 carrot
4 swede
5 turnip
6 parsnip
7 radish

Choosing and storing

Choose firm, well-shaped root vegetables and potatoes with no soft patches or sproutings. Potatoes should have no green patches on their skins. These vegetables have good keeping qualities and will last a week or two. Remove plastic packaging and store the vegetables loose, preferably in a vegetable rack in a cold, dark, airy place.

 Root vegetables keep well in the ground and some can even survive frost. Once pulled up, the stems and leaves are discarded and, in most root vegetables, the root is peeled and chopped.

 FOOD FACTS

Carrots and other yellow or orange foods contain a chemical called beta carotene. This works in the body like a vitamin, protecting it from harm.

Mashed potato

SERVES: 2	PREPARATION TIME: 10 MINUTES	COOKING TIME: 20 MINUTES

Although this is a classic recipe for mashed potato, it can be used for root vegetables and other tubers or a combination of them.

Ingredients
2 medium potatoes
1 tablespoon butter
2 tablespoons milk
salt and pepper

1. Half fill a medium-sized saucepan with water. Bring the water to the boil. In the meantime, peel and wash the potatoes. Cut them into small pieces.

2. When the water is boiling rapidly, add the potatoes. Allow them to boil for about 20 minutes until they are soft.

3. Use a colander to drain the potatoes, then put them back into the saucepan.

4. Add the butter and milk to the potatoes and mash with a potato masher or fork until the potatoes are smooth and soft. Season with salt and pepper to taste.

Pommes Dauphinoise

This rich and creamy potato dish will go well with any meat recipe.

Ingredients
600g Maris Piper potatoes
350ml milk
350ml double cream
1 large garlic clove, peeled and finely chopped
salt and pepper
100g Gruyere cheese, grated

1. Preheat the oven to 200°C/ gas mark 6.

2. Peel and slice the potatoes thinly.

3. Put the milk and cream in a saucepan and bring the mixture to the boil.

4. Add the garlic, salt and pepper to taste and simmer for 5 minutes.

5. Add the potato slices and stir gently. Simmer for about 10 minutes, until the potatoes are just tender.

6. Drain the potatoes in a colander, but catch the creamy milk in the saucepan or another bowl.

7. Cover the bottom of an ovenproof dish in potato slices. Sprinkle some of the grated Gruyere cheese over the layer of potatoes and add a little of the creamy milk. Repeat this until all the potatoes are in layers and you have used up two-thirds of the cheese.

8. Pour a little of the milk around the sides, just enough to slightly cover the potatoes. Sprinkle over the last third of the cheese.

10. Bake in the oven for about 25 minutes until the cheese starts to bubble and turns a golden brown.

11. Allow to stand for 10 minutes before serving.

COOK'S TIP

Mature Cheddar cheese can be used instead of the Gruyere.

Borscht

SERVES: 4	PREPARATION TIME: 20 MINUTES	COOKING TIME: 30 MINUTES

This traditional Polish soup is often served with dumplings.

Ingredients:
1 celeriac
1 carrot
1 onion
1 parsnip
900ml water
2 beetroot
2 garlic cloves, peeled and finely chopped
juice of 1 lemon
1 teaspoon sugar
salt and pepper
crème fraiche, to serve

1. Peel and chop all the vegetables very finely.

2. Put the water in a saucepan and bring it to the boil. Add the chopped vegetables and allow to boil for 20–30 minutes, until the vegetables are tender.

3. Without draining the vegetables, put them into a food processor and whizz them to make a smooth purée.

4. Return the soup to the heat and add the garlic, lemon juice and sugar and season to taste.

5. Ladle the soup into serving bowls. Serve with a dollop of crème fraiche.

Sweet potato soup

SERVES: 4	PREPARATION TIME: 20 MINUTES	COOKING TIME: 20 MINUTES

This soup is delicious served with heated naan or pitta bread.

Ingredients
1 tablespoon sunflower oil
1 onion, peeled and finely chopped
1 garlic clove, peeled and finely chopped
750g sweet potatoes, peeled and grated
1 vegetable stock cube mixed with 1 litre water
50ml double cream
salt and pepper
fresh coriander, to serve

1. Heat the oil in a large saucepan and fry the onion and garlic for 2–3 minutes.

2. Add the sweet potatoes and stock and bring to the boil. Allow to simmer for 15 minutes, until the potatoes are soft.

3. Remove from the heat and stir in the cream and seasoning to taste.

4. Use a food processor to make the soup smooth.

5. Sprinkle with fresh coriander to serve.

Green vegetables

Cabbage, broccoli, spinach and cauliflower are some of the powerhouses of the vegetable kingdom. They are packed with vitamins and other disease-fighting nutrients.

Why eat greens?

Green vegetables are bursting with antioxidants, which help to prevent disease, and folic acid, which encourages healthy blood cells. Greens also contain minerals, including calcium, which helps to strengthen and repair bones and teeth; magnesium, which helps the body to release energy from food; and iron, which builds up red blood cells.

FOOD FACTS

Dark, leafy spinach is packed with nutrients that benefit our digestive system, nerve function, skin and sight. Kale and chard are other leafy greens that contain similar nutrients.

A selection of green vegetables:

1 white cabbage	4 lettuce
2 spinach	5 broccoli
3 pak choi	6 cauliflower

Where are greens eaten?

Green vegetables are eaten wherever they will grow and are the basis of many famous dishes. In central and Eastern Europe, cabbage leaves are stuffed with rice, meat and flavourings to make a hearty dish. Spinach is often served with eggs, for example in eggs Florentine, a well-known Italian dish. Elsewhere in southern Europe, peas and beans are often cooked in olive oil with garlic, onion and or diced cured ham. Pak choi and similar greens are essential ingredients in China and the Far East, where they are quickly wilted over the heat of a stove and served with stir-fries.

Cooking broccoli in a steamer above a pan of boiling water helps to preserve its nutrients.

are all better than boiling. Some greens, such as endives, can be baked in the oven. Cauliflower is often served with a cheese sauce. Most green vegetables are best served young, when they are sweet and tasty. The pods of peas and beans can then be eaten, too, and make delicious early summer soups.

How are greens cooked?

Many green vegetables require very little cooking, which helps to preserve the nutrients they contain. Nutrients are easily destroyed in cooking, so it is good to eat greens raw in salads or to cook them briefly in as little liquid as possible. Steaming, stir-frying and microwaving

Choosing and storing greens

Choose vegetables that are bright green, firm and undamaged. Avoid greens that look limp or yellow. Greens are best stored in a cool, dark, dry place, preferably the fridge, for two to three days. Always eat them while they are fresh, as soon as possible after buying. All green vegetables need to be washed thoroughly before using.

Cooked cabbage

SERVES: 2–3 | **PREPARATION TIME: 10 MINUTES** | **COOKING TIME: 10 MINUTES**

This simple method of cooking can be used for most green vegetables.

Ingredients
1 small cabbage, cut in half
1 knob of butter
salt and pepper

1. Half fill a saucepan with water and bring it to the boil.

2. In the meantime, cut out the middle stem of the cabbage as this is hard and will not cook or soften.

3. Chop the cabbage into strips and then again, so that the cabbage is in small pieces.

4. Wash the cabbage thoroughly. Shake off the water and add it to the boiling water. Allow it to cook for 10 minutes.

5. Use a colander to drain off the water and put the cabbage back in the saucepan.

6. Add the butter and salt and pepper to taste before serving.

 COOK'S TIP

The water that is drained off the cabbage or other green vegetables contains a lot of Vitamin C and can be used to make a gravy.

Eggs Florentine

Poached egg is perfectly teamed with the wilted spinach in this Italian dish.

Ingredients
50g fresh spinach
1 egg
1 teaspoon white vinegar
2 slices ciabatta bread
2 teaspoons olive oil
salt and pepper

1. Chop up the spinach and put it into a colander. Place the colander under cold water. Dry the spinach on a clean kitchen towel.

2. Crack the egg into a bowl.

3. Half fill a small saucepan with water and bring it to the boil.

4. When the water is boiling, rapidly add the vinegar. Turn the water down to a simmer and stir it. When the water is swirling, add the egg and allow it poach for 2–3 minutes.

5. In the meantime preheat the grill if it is electric. Brush the bread with a little oil and place it under the grill to toast.

6. Keeping an eye on the bread, place the spinach in a pan with the rest of the oil and cook on a moderate heat for 1 minute.

7. When the toast is ready, place it on a plate, then add the spinach and the egg on top of it.

8. Season with salt and pepper before serving.

COOK'S TIP

Wholewheat bread can be used instead of ciabatta. It has more fibre than ciabatta so it is healthier.

Broccoli beef noodles

SERVES: 2   **PREPARATION TIME: 15 MINUTES**   **COOKING TIME: 15 MINUTES**

This noodle dish is quick and easy to cook. If you prefer a milder flavour, you can leave out the red chilli.

Ingredients
200g rump or frying steak
1 bunch broccoli
1 red chilli, deseeded
1 tablespoon oil
150ml oyster sauce
150g straight-to-wok
   noodles

1. Slice the beef into thin strips.

2. Chop the broccoli and chilli into bite-size pieces.

3. Heat the oil in a wok and add the beef and oyster sauce. Fry until there is no pink meat left on the beef.

4. Add the broccoli and chilli to the meat and stir well. Cook for 5 minutes, adding a little water if the mixture is dry.

5. Add the noodles and cook for 2–3 minutes. Serve piping hot.

Broad beans and ham

SERVES: 2   **PREPARATION TIME: 15 MINUTES**   **COOKING TIME: 25 MINUTES**

This colourful dish makes a great side dish or main meal on its own.

Ingredients
900g broad beans
50ml olive oil
100g Serrano ham,
   diced
2 garlic cloves, peeled
   and finely chopped
salt and pepper
1 tablespoon chopped parsley,
   to serve

1. Shell and skin the beans, leaving a brilliant, green bean.

2. In a pan, heat the oil and fry the beans, ham and garlic on a high heat for 3–4 minutes.

3. Reduce the heat and cook for 20 minutes, until the beans are soft.

4. Season to taste and add the parsley before serving.

Vegetable fruits

Vegetable fruits come in many different shapes, sizes and colours, and are rich in tastes and textures. From avocados and squash to cucumbers and peppers, these fleshy foods are a good source of nutrition and provide us with a taste of summer all the year round.

Why eat vegetable fruits?

These colourful vegetables are packed with goodness. For example, peppers contain large amounts of Vitamin C, which helps to heal wounds and prevent infection. Pumpkins and other squashes contain important minerals, such as potassium, which helps the heart, kidneys and digestive system. Tomatoes contain a powerful antioxidant, known as lycopene, which helps to fight disease.

Where are they eaten?

Vegetable fruits are eaten all over the world. Peppers and chillis are popular in Mexico and the south-western USA, where they put the heat into salsa.

In southern Europe, tomatoes, courgettes, aubergines and peppers are used to make a stew, known as *ratatouille*. Aubergines are important in Greece and the Middle East, where they are combined with minced lamb in *moussaka*. Pumpkins are associated with the United States. At Halloween they are hollowed out and carved into lanterns. In the following month, they are made into a sweet pie and served at Thanksgiving dinner.

FOOD FACTS

Red, yellow and orange peppers all start out as green peppers but change colour as they ripen. Chillies are a hot pepper and add heat to food.

A selection of vegetable fruits

1 peppers	5 courgette	8 avocado pear
2 butternut squash	6 cherry tomatoes	9 tomato
3 acorn squash	7 chilli	10 cucumber
4 aubergine		

How are they eaten?

Vegetable fruits are best grilled or roasted, which preserves and intensifies their flavour. Since many of these vegetables are large and sturdy, they can be hollowed out and filled with stuffings made of meat, rice, breadcrumbs, cheese or herbs. Tomatoes can be simmered to make sauces for pasta, pizza or meatballs. They can also be eaten raw in salads, along with cucumber, avocado and peppers. Squashes are delicious roasted or stuffed or used to make soups, risottos or pies.

 Traditionally, pumpkins are carved into lanterns at Halloween and the flesh is used to make a pumpkin pie.

Ratatouille

SERVES: 2   **PREPARATION TIME: 20 MINUTES**   **COOKING TIME: 30 MINUTES**

This dish can be served as an accompaniment to a main meal or with warm bread as a main meal in its own right.

Ingredients
2 aubergines, cut into cubes
2 courgettes, cut into slices
   1 cm thick
2 tablespoons oil
1 onion, peeled and finely chopped
1 garlic clove, peeled and
   finely chopped
400g tin chopped tomatoes
1 tablespoon fresh basil,
   finely chopped
salt and pepper
bread, to serve

1. Place the aubergines and courgettes in a colander. Sprinkle salt over them and cover them with a plate. Leave them to stand.

2. Heat the oil in a saucepan and fry the onion and garlic until the onion changes colour but before it turns brown.

3. Rinse the aubergines and courgettes. Add them and the tomatoes to the saucepan and stir well. Leave to simmer for 30 minutes. Before serving, add the fresh basil.

 COOK'S TIP

If you use fresh tomatoes instead of tinned, you will need to skin them first (see page 47).

Pumpkin pie

Shortcrust pastry filled with mouthwatering pumpkin is perfect for Thanksgiving, served with custard or crème fraiche.

Ingredients
sunflower oil, for greasing
300g pumpkin flesh cut into cubes
1 egg
50g soft brown sugar
1 teaspoon cinnamon
140ml double cream

For the pastry
100g white plain flour, plus extra
    for sprinkling
50g butter
6 teaspoons cold water

1. Preheat the oven to 190°C/gas mark 5. Lightly grease a 20cm pie dish with oil.

2. Half fill a saucepan with water and bring it to the boil. Add the chopped pumpkin and cook it for 10 minutes.

3. In the meantime, make the pastry. Rub the butter into the flour until it resembles fine breadcrumbs. (see page 47).

4. Use a metal spoon to stir in the cold water and mix well to make a soft dough.

5. Sprinkle flour onto the work surface. Roll out the pastry so that it is large enough to line the bottom and sides of the pie dish. Set aside.

6. When the pumpkin is cooked, drain it in a colander and mash it as it as it finely as possible.

7. Whisk the egg in a bowl and set it aside.

8. Place the sugar, cinnamon and cream in a saucepan and allow it to simmer. Whisk it to mix well.

9. Pour the mixture over the egg and whisk well.

10. Add the pumpkin to the cream mixture and stir well.

11. Put the filling into the pastry and bake for 35–40 minutes until the centre is slightly wobbly but the edges are puffed up.

COOK'S TIP

If you cannot find pumpkin, you could use butternut squash instead.

Caponata

SERVES: 2　　**PREPARATION TIME: 20 MINUTES**　　**COOKING TIME: 40 MINUTES**

This traditional Sicilian dish can be served hot or cold.

Ingredients
2 aubergines, diced
1 onion
2 celery sticks
2 tablespoons sunflower oil
400g tinned tomatoes
100g green olives
50g capers
1 tablespoon sugar
30ml red wine vinegar
1 tablespoon parsley,
　chopped, to serve
salt and pepper

1. Sprinkle the aubergines with salt and allow to stand.

2. In the meantime, peel and chop the onion and celery.

3. Rinse the aubergines and pat them dry with kitchen towel.

4. Heat the oil in a frying pan and fry the aubergines for about 10 minutes. Set them aside.

5. Fry the onions and celery until the onions are soft. Add the tomatoes and stir well. Add the olives and allow to simmer for 20 minutes.

6. Add the aubergines and capers to the pan and stir well. In a bowl, combine the sugar and vinegar and add them to the pan. Allow to cook for 10 minutes.

7. Sprinkle with the parsley and season to taste before serving.

Stuffed peppers

SERVES: 2　　**PREPARATION TIME: 20 MINUTES**　　**COOKING TIME: 10 MINUTES**

This quick and easy recipe is great as a lunchtime meal on a cold winter's day.

Ingredients
2 red peppers
100g cooked rice
1 tablespoon green pesto
4 pitted black
　olives, chopped
100g goat's cheese, sliced

1. Cut the top off the peppers, then scoop out the seeds and pith. These insides can be thrown away.

2. Put the peppers on a plate cut side up. Cook in a microwave oven on high for 5 minutes, until they have wilted and are soft.

3. While the peppers are cooking, mix the rice with the pesto, olives and two-thirds of the cheese.

4. When the peppers are cooked, spoon the rice mixture into the peppers and top with the remaining cheese.

6. Return the peppers to the microwave oven and cook for a further 5 minutes on high so that the cheese melts.

Legumes and pulses

Healthy and versatile, legumes and pulses come in a variety of colours, shapes, and flavours. Easy to cook and tasty to eat, they add a filling texture and make many delicious dishes.

Fresh, tinned or frozen

This vegetable group includes fresh peas and beans, which grow in long, green pods. If the pods are thoroughly dried, their round or oval seeds can be shelled and stored for future use. They are known as pulses.

Why eat pulses?

Legumes and pulses are rich in proteins and, when eaten with grains, form the same high-quality proteins as those found in meat and fish. This makes legumes and pulses invaluable for vegetarians. They are a good source of fibre, carbohydrates, vitamins and minerals, including iron. Because legumes and pulses are complex carbohydrates, they release their sugars gradually, which makes them useful for diabetics, who need to keep their sugar levels constant. With the exception of soya beans, legumes and pulses are low in fat.

How are legumes and pulses eaten?

Peas and beans can be eaten in different ways. Some peas are removed from the pod, while others, such as mangetout and snap peas, are eaten pod and all. They are very good in stir-fries. Broad beans are removed from the pod, but with most beans the pod is eaten too – either whole or cut into slices.

Pulses can be eaten as a side vegetable and they are often combined with other foods in soups, stews, casseroles and curries.

 Fresh peas and beans (top) are delicious in season. Their dried seeds (middle) are known as pulses. Dried pulses need to be soaked and cooked, but are also available tinned (bottom).

In India, *dhal*, made from lentils, is a staple food. In the Middle East, people enjoy dipping warm pitta bread in a purée of chickpeas, olive oil and garlic, which is known as houmous.

Soya
Soya beans are rich in fats and contain twice as much protein as other legumes. They can be processed to make soya milk and tofu, which is a firm curd that is widely used in Asian food.

Choosing and storing pulses
Choose legumes with a deep, glossy colour, avoiding any that look faded. They should be stored in a fridge. Pulses need to be stored in an airtight container away from heat, light and moisture. They will keep fresh for up to a year. Many pulses need to be soaked overnight, and then boiled for up to an hour or more. Fortunately, many legumes are available canned and ready to eat.

 Tofu, also known as bean curd, is made from soya milk, which is produced from soya beans. Tofu has very little taste of its own but absorbs the flavours of other ingredients.

Houmous

SERVES: 2	PREPARATION TIME: 10 MINUTES	COOKING TIME: NO COOKING

This Middle Eastern dip is often served with warmed pitta bread and black olives. The chickpeas are a good source of protein.

Ingredients
400g tin chickpeas, rinsed and drained
1 garlic clove, peeled and finely chopped
1 tablespoon lemon juice
1 tablespoon olive oil
1 tablespoon tahini (sesame seed paste)
salt and pepper
pitta bread and olives, to serve

1. Put all the ingredients, except the salt and pepper, in a large bowl or food processor and mash or blend to a smooth consistency.

2. Add salt and pepper to taste. Blend again. Serve with warm pitta bread and olives.

COOK'S TIP

Dried chickpeas can be used, but they need to be soaked overnight and boiled for about two hours before using.

Lentil dhal

SERVES: 4   PREPARATION TIME: 20 MINUTES   COOKING TIME: 50 MINUTES

This traditional Indian dish is delicious served with mango chutney.

Ingredients
60ml sunflower oil
1 teaspoon cumin seeds
1 teaspoon coriander seeds
¼ teaspoon turmeric
1 onion, peeled and finely chopped
1 garlic clove, peeled and finely chopped
200g red lentils
1 litre water
150g runner beans
4 tomatoes

1. Heat half of the oil in a large saucepan. Add the spice seeds and fry them for 2 minutes.

2. Remove the spices from the pan and put them in a mortar and pestle. Crush them.

3. Using the same pan, heat the remaining oil and fry the onion and garlic for 2 minutes.

4. Add the spices and stir well. Cook for another 2 minutes.

5. Add the lentils and water. Bring to the boil, then allow to simmer for 40 minutes. If the mixture becomes dry, add more water.

6. In the meantime, prepare the runner beans by trimming the ends and cutting them into pieces 5mm long.

7. Cut the tomatoes into small, bite-sized pieces.

8. When the lentils are soft, add the beans and tomatoes and cook the dhal for a further 5 minutes.

COOK'S TIP

Add a fresh chilli or chilli powder for some heat.

Tuna and bean salad

SERVES: 2 | **PREPARATION TIME: 20 MINUTES** | **COOKING TIME: NO COOKING**

This salad is packed with lots of beans, giving you all the protein you need.

Ingredients

100g frozen runner beans, thawed
185g tin tuna, drained
400g tin cannelloni beans, drained
1 red onion, peeled and chopped
1 tablespoon olive oil
1 tablespoon lemon juice
2 garlic cloves, peeled and chopped
2 tablespoons Parmesan cheese, grated
salt and pepper

1. Put all the ingredients in a large bowl. Season to taste and mix well.

2. Cover with cling film and refrigerate for about an hour before serving.

COOK'S TIP

Fresh runner beans can be used, but they need to be blanched (see page 47) before adding them to the other ingredients.

Minestrone soup

SERVES: 4–6 | **PREPARATION TIME: 25 MINUTES** | **COOKING TIME: 1 HOUR 15 MINUTES**

This hearty Italian soup makes an ideal meal on a cold winter's day.

Ingredients

1 tablespoon oil
1 onion, peeled and chopped
1 garlic clove, peeled and finely chopped
2 litres water
50g haricot beans
2 carrots, peeled and diced
2 celery sticks, chopped
2 potatoes, peeled and diced
2 courgettes, chopped
4 tomatoes, chopped
50g small macaroni
1 tablespoon chopped parsley
50g shavings Parmesan cheese

1. Heat the oil in a large saucepan. Fry the onion and garlic until they change colour, but not until they are brown.

2. Add the water and haricot beans and bring to the boil. Allow to simmer for 15 minutes.

3. Add all the other vegetables, bring the mixture back to the boil and then simmer for 45 minutes.

4. Add the macaroni and cook for a further 15 minutes.

5. Stir in the parsley and serve with the shavings of Parmesan cheese.

Orchard fruits

There is an old saying that "an apple a day keeps the doctor away." The same could be said of the other orchard fruits, such as plums and pears. These healthy foods are good for snacking and are also used in drinks and desserts.

What are orchard fruits?

Orchard fruits include apples, apricots, cherries, pears, plums, quinces, peaches and nectarines. Each group includes many different varieties. In the United Kingdom alone, for example, there are nearly 2,000 different varieties of apple, ranging from small, sweet dessert apples to larger, sharper cooking varieties.

Why eat orchard fruits?

Orchard fruits are an important part of a healthy diet. They are packed with antioxidants – vitamins that destroy harmful substances in the body that can build up and cause disease. They also contain important minerals and are fat free. Eaten with their skins on, they are a great source of fibre, which is important to keep our digestion working properly.

How do they grow?

Apples, pears and plums grow in cool, temperate places, while apricots, peaches and nectarines require a warmer climate. In spring, the fruit trees are covered in blossom, which attracts bees and other insects. As the insects feed on the sweet-smelling nectar, they pollinate the flowers, enabling the fruits to develop. Throughout the summer, the fruit swells and ripens. The earliest varieties are harvested in midsummer; the latest in early autumn. There are dozens of different ways to make use of the seasonal harvest.

 Apples, pears and plums have sweet, juicy flesh, which surrounds the seeds or 'stone'. All of these fruits make healthy snacks.

How are they eaten?

Most orchard fruits are delicious eaten raw. Apples are particularly good for snacking because they are robust and less likely to bruise when carried around. The fruit can also be chopped on muesli or cereals or added to salads.

FOOD FACTS

To meet one of your five-a-day portions, just eat one apple, peach or pear, two plums, three apricots or a small bowl of cherries.

Unlike most fruit, pears need to be harvested before they are ready to eat, usually in late summer. The fruit ripens about one to two weeks after picking.

Orchard fruits can also be cooked. This softens them and changes their flavour. They can be stewed and served in pies and crumbles, added to cakes or simply baked. Apples appear in many famous recipes such as *apple pie* or *Dutch apple cake*. Pears may be stewed in wine or cooked and coated with chocolate sauce, as in the French dessert *Belle Helene*. Baked peaches are used in *Peach Melba*, alongside ice cream and raspberry sauce.

Processing the fruit

Most orchard fruits can be turned into juices, ciders and other drinks or preserved in chutneys. The fruit can also be preserved by drying. Dried apricots make a tasty snack and are especially good when soaked and cooked, and then served in a syrup. Dried cherries are used in cakes and mince pies.

Orchard fruit crumble

| SERVES: 2 | PREPARATION TIME: 30 MINUTES | COOKING TIME: 20 MINUTES |

This twist on apple crumble uses pears and plums. It can be served with cream, ice cream or custard.

Ingredients
50g margarine or butter
100g plain white flour
50g sugar
50g rolled oats
1 pear, peeled
1 plum
2 tablespoons water

1. Preheat the oven to 180°C/gas mark 4.

2. Rub the margarine or butter into the flour until the mixture resembles fine breadcrumbs (see page 47).

3. Stir in the sugar and oats.

4. Cut the fruit into small cubes so that they resemble dice. Place them in a small ovenproof dish and add the water.

5. Sprinkle over the crumble mixture and bake in the oven for 20 minutes.

Dutch apple cake

| SERVES: 2 | PREPARATION TIME: 30 MINUTES | COOKING TIME: 20 MINUTES |

This cake makes a perfect tea-time treat when served with fresh cream.

Ingredients
65g butter, plus extra for greasing
175g caster sugar
1 medium egg
125g plain flour
½ teaspoon baking powder
1 teaspoon ground nutmeg
350g apples, peeled and diced
whipped cream, to serve

1. Preheat the oven to 180°C/ gas mark 4.

2. Cream together the butter and sugar.

3. Add the egg and mix well.

4. Add the flour, baking powder and nutmeg and stir to make a smooth batter.

5. Add the apples and mix well.

6. Pour the mixture into an 18cm greased tin. Bake for 1 hour and 15 minutes.

7. Lower the temperature to 150°C/ gas mark 2 and bake for 20 minutes. Remove from the oven and leave to cool on a wire rack before serving.

Peach Melba

| SERVES: 2 | PREPARATION TIME: 30 MINUTES | COOKING TIME: 5 MINUTES |

This recipe is named after the Australian opera singer Dame Nellie Melba and is a favourite with adults and children alike.

Ingredients
2 egg whites
1 tablespoon caster sugar
142ml double cream
1 drop vanilla essence
1 peach, stone removed

COOK'S TIP

If you over-whisk the cream, clots will form and it will look like cottage cheese.

1. Whisk the egg whites until they form soft peaks. Add the sugar and whisk until stiff peaks form.

2. Place the cream and vanilla essence in a separate bowl and whisk until thick.

3. Divide the cream into two servings and put a peach half on top of each one.

4. Spoon the egg whites into a piping bag and pipe them over each peach half in a spiral shape.

5. Carefully use a blow torch to glaze the meringue until golden brown. Serve immediately.

Poached pears with chocolate sauce

SERVES: 2 **PREPARATION TIME: 30 MINUTES** **COOKING TIME: 30 MINUTES**

This traditional French recipe is called Poires Belle Helene. It can be served with a scoop of rich vanilla ice cream.

Ingredients
2 pears, peeled but with the stalk
   in tact
375ml water
375g sugar

For the chocolate sauce
250ml double cream
300g milk chocolate, broken
   into pieces

1. Cut the pears in half lengthways and remove the core. Slice the bottom off each half to make a flat base.

2. Place the pears upright in a pan with the water and sugar and cook for 20 minutes, until tender but firm enough to stand up.

3. In the meantime, to make the chocolate sauce, put the cream in saucepan on a low heat. Add the chocolate pieces and heat until the chocolate has melted. Stir well.

4. Remove the pears from the pan, keeping the syrup. Place each one standing up on a serving plate.

5. Add a tablespoon of the syrup to the chocolate sauce and stir well.

6. Pour the chocolate sauce over the pears and serve.

COOK'S TIP

Use a potato peeler to peel the pears.

Berries and currants

Strawberries, raspberries, blackcurrants – we associate these sweet, deep-coloured fruit with warm summer days. While many of them are delicious raw, they can also be used to make mouth-watering desserts.

 Berries come in different sizes and colours. From left to right: blackberries, strawberries, blueberries, raspberries.

What are berries and currants?

Berries and currants are the fruit of certain flowering plants, which have been bred to produce tasty fruit. Berry fruits grown in gardens and on farms include strawberries, raspberries, loganberries, tayberries, cranberries, gooseberries and blueberries. Raspberries are grown on tall canes, while strawberries are grown in beds on the ground, surrounded by straw to keep the fruit clean. Blueberries and cranberries grow in cooler places and prefer boggy ground. Currants are small and round in shape and can be black, red or white. These fruits come in many different varieties, each one slightly different in its appearance, flavour or fruiting time. Currants grow best in full sun.

Why eat berries and currants?

Berry fruits are often called 'super foods' because of their nutritional goodness. Like many other colourful foods, they are rich in antioxidants that destroy harmful substances in the body, which can build up and cause cancers. The fruits are particularly rich in Vitamin C, boosting the immune system in the fight against disease. Aside from their nutritional content, the soft fruits are easy to serve and require little preparation. Best of all, they taste delicious.

 FOOD FACTS

One 150ml serving of cranberry juice contains many disease-busting nutrients, including the recommended daily requirement for Vitamin C. Doctors routinely recommend the juice to people who suffer from bladder infections.

Choosing and storing berry fruit

Berries and currants are highly perishable, so they need to be used within a few days of purchase. Choose perfect-looking fruit and store in the fridge. Always wash the fruit before eating or using it in recipes.

How are they eaten?

All berries can be eaten raw, added to cereals and smoothies, or served with yoghurt, ice cream or cream. In the Australian dessert, raspberry pavlova, fresh raspberries are served on a thick meringue base, while strawberries and cream are a traditional English favourite.

Currants are too sharp for eating raw and should be gently cooked and sweetened with sugar. They can then be used in crumbles and pies, or puréed and sieved to make sauces and coulis. At the height of the season, all of these fruits can be preserved by boiling with sugar to make jams and jellies. Some are used to make juices or liqueurs. Blackcurrant juice is popular with children, while in France the fruit is used to create Cassis, a popular liqueur.

 Strawberries are grown in beds on sunny, well-drained soil. In late spring, straw is laid under the plants to prevent the growing fruit from touching the ground. Strawberries need to be picked as soon as they are ripe to prevent them rotting.

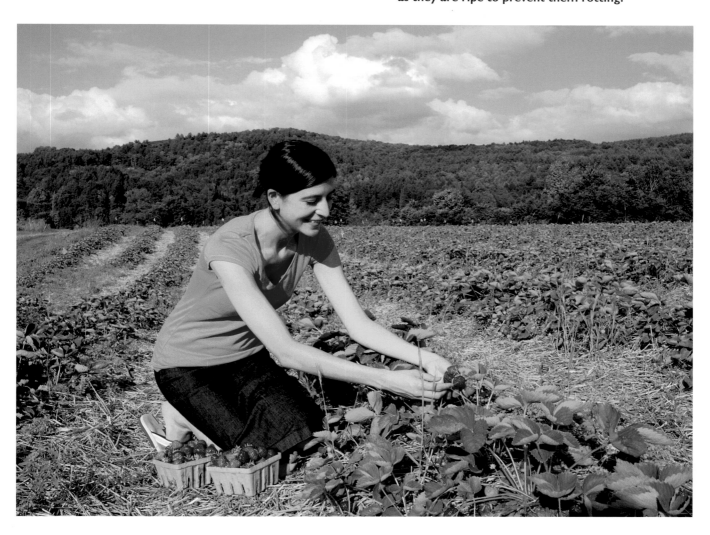

Summer pudding

This summer pudding uses a mix of different berries to create a mouth-watering dessert.

Ingredients
2 tablespoons water
150g sugar
450g mixed berries
4–6 slices of white bread
whipped cream, to serve

1. Put the water and sugar in a saucepan and bring to the boil.

2. Add the fruits and stew gently until they are soft but still have their shape.

3. Cut the crusts off the bread. Line a 900ml pudding basin with the bread.

4. Pour in the fruit and cover with more slices of bread.

5. Place a saucer with a weight on it on top of the pudding and leave it overnight in the fridge.

6. Turn out the pudding and serve with the cream.

COOK'S TIP

You can make miniature summer puddings by using small ramekins instead of one big pudding bowl.

Strawberry foam

This light and fluffy strawberry mousse is perfect on a hot summer's day.

Ingredients
225g ripe strawberries
1 egg white
75g icing sugar

1. Remove the stems from the strawberries and put them in a large mixing bowl.

2. Reserve two strawberries for serving. Mash the remaining strawberries until smooth.

3. Add the egg white and icing sugar to the strawberries. Whisk for about 10 minutes until the mixture is thick and frothy.

4. Pile the mixture into glasses and chill until ready to serve. Before serving, garnish with the two reserved strawberries.

Raspberry pavlova

SERVES: 6 **PREPARATION TIME: 40 MINUTES** **COOKING TIME: 1 HOUR**

This delicious berry dessert never fails to impress people.

Ingredients
3 egg whites
175g caster sugar
5g cornflour
½ teaspoon vinegar
284ml double cream
250g fresh raspberries
icing sugar, to serve

1. Preheat the oven to 150°C/ gas mark 2.

2. Draw a circle 18cm in diameter on baking paper and place the paper on a baking tray.

3. Whisk the egg whites until they are stiff. Add the sugar a little at a time and whisk.

4. Add the cornflour and vinegar and whisk until the egg whites are very stiff and shiny. You should be able to turn the bowl upside down without the mixture moving.

5. Spread the meringue mixture over the circle of baking paper and bake for about 1 hour until the meringue is firm.

6. When cooked, remove the meringue from the oven and allow to cool before transferring it to a flat plate.

7. Whisk the cream until thick and pile it on top of the meringue. Arrange the raspberries on top of the meringue, dust with icing sugar and serve.

COOK'S TIP

You could use strawberries, blackberries, blueberries or a combination of them instead of raspberries.

Citrus fruits

Most of us enjoy a squeeze of lemon on warm pancakes or a glass of orange juice to start the day. Citrus fruits are full of tangy juice with a delicious fruity flavour. They help to cleanse the system and give us some get-up-and-go!

What are the citrus fruits?

Citrus fruits include oranges, lemons, limes, grapefruit, satsumas, mandarins, pomelos and tangerines. The fruit grows in segments with a thin, edible skin, called the pith. Each fruit is surrounded by a thick peel, which has to be removed before eating. The fruits grow in groves or orchards in places with a sub-tropical climate, such as Brazil, California, Spain and South Africa. The fruits develop in the summer, ripen in the autumn and are harvested during the winter.

Why eat citrus fruits?

Citrus fruits are extremely healthy and contain large amounts of fibre, minerals and vitamins, notably Vitamin C. Their high dosage of Vitamin C means that eating them regularly can help to prevent colds and flu. The fruits are all acidic and are excellent at helping to get rid of toxins (the harmful chemicals that our bodies absorb from fumes, cleaning products, fertilisers and pesticides). Toxins are believed to contribute to disease and can cause a lack of energy.

 Citrus fruits are bursting with juice. Clockwise from top left: lime, grapefruit, lemon, orange.

 FOOD FACTS

A glass of orange juice counts as only one portion of fruit. Eating whole fruit is much more nutritious.

FOOD FACTS

A mandarin is a type of small orange with a loose skin. A tangerine is a type of mandarin with a red-orange skin. A clementine is a seedless mandarin. A satsuma is similar to a clementine but has a tighter skin.

How are they eaten?

Oranges, mandarins, clementines and satsumas are all sweet enough to be eaten raw. They are portable and easy to peel. An orange flavour goes well with chocolate and so orange juice or zest is often added to cakes and desserts. Grapefruits are often eaten before a meal, usually breakfast, because their sharper juice cleanses the palate and stimulates the body's digestive juices. Lemons are mainly used in cooking and to make popular desserts such as lemon sorbet and lemon meringue pie. In Morocco, they are preserved in salt to add flavour to local stews called tagines. Lime, which is both tangy and sweet, is widely used in Thai cooking, which is full of lively flavours.

Processing the fruit

Much of the world's vast citrus harvest is turned into juice and shipped around the world. The juice is also added to iced lollies, lemonade and fruit squashes. Lemons can be used to make lemon curd, while sour oranges (known as Sevilles) are boiled with sugar to make marmalade – a jam-like staple of the traditional British breakfast.

 Like all citrus fruits, oranges are green at first but change colour as they ripen. Once ripe, the fruit can stay on the tree for weeks or months before it is picked.

Lemon sorbet

Refreshing, tangy and ice-cold, lemon sorbet makes a great alternative to ice cream after a main meal.

Ingredients
100g caster sugar
300ml water
juice of 3 lemons
zest of one lemon
2 egg whites

1. Put the sugar and water in a saucepan over a low heat. Bring to the boil and allow to simmer for 10 minutes.

2. Add a tablespoon of the lemon juice and stir.

3. Put the zest in a bowl and pour over the hot syrup. Leave to cool.

4. When cold, add the remaining lemon juice and mix well.

5. Put the mixture in a sealed tub in the freezer until it is a slush-like consistency.

6. Whisk the egg whites until they are stiff, then fold them into the lemon slush.

7. Put the sorbet back in the freezer until the ice sets. Serve in tall glasses or bowls.

COOK'S TIP

Use oranges or grapefruit instead of lemons – or a combination of all three for a zesty sorbet.

Satsuma cup cakes

| SERVES: 12 | PREPARATION TIME: 30 MINUTES | COOKING TIME: 20 MINUTES |

The light sponge and sweet satsuma of this recipe combine to make delicious cup cakes.

Ingredients
2 satsumas
100g all purpose flour
½ teaspoon baking powder
100g caster sugar
100g margarine
2 eggs
icing sugar, to serve

1. Preheat the oven to 180°C/gas mark 4. Line a 12-hole muffin tray with paper cases.

2. Peel the satsumas and chop them into very small pieces. Set aside.

3. Place the flour, baking powder, sugar, margarine and eggs in a bowl and mix together until the mixture makes a creamy mousse.

4. Add the satsuma pieces and mix well.

5. Spread the mixture out evenly into the cupcake cases.

6. Bake for 20 minutes. Remove from the oven and leave to cool on a wire rack before dusting with icing sugar.

COOK'S TIP

You can tell when the cupcakes are ready because the sponge will bounce back when you touch it.

Citrus wake up

| SERVES: 4 | PREPARATION TIME: 30 MINUTES | COOKING TIME: NO COOKING |

This drink is packed with Vitamin C and so it is a great, healthy way to start your day.

Ingredients
4 oranges
1 red grapefruit
1 lemon
1 lime
zest of one lime
100ml water
1 tablespoon caster sugar
2 tablespoons fresh mint, shredded
lemon or orange slices, to serve

1. Cut the oranges, grapefruit, lemon and lime in half around the centre.

2. Use a hand juicer to squeeze out all the juice from the fruits.

3. Combine the juices with the lime zest, water, sugar and mint.

4. Pour the juice into glasses. Serve with a slice of lemon or orange.

Tropical fruits

Many of the most delicious fruits grow in the tropics – the warmest, wettest parts of the world. Due to air-freighting, they are now transported all over the world and people who live in cooler places can enjoy them, too.

 A plateful of tropical flavour. Clockwise from left: passion fruit, papaya, mango, pineapple, lychee, banana.

How and where do they grow?

Bananas and pineapples are the fruit of herbaceous plants, which are grown throughout the tropics. Lychees, mangoes and papayas grow on trees. Lychees, which are called the cherries of Asia, are found in China, Vietnam, Pakistan, India, Bangladesh and other parts of Asia. Passion fruit and kiwis grow on woody vines. Passion fruit is found through the topics but particularly in South America and South Africa, while kiwis, which originated in China, are now also grown in New Zealand and Italy.

Eating tropical fruits

Most tropical fruits have a delicious aroma and flavour and they make excellent desserts. They are nutritional powerhouses, packed with vitamins and minerals, such as iron and potassium, and adding plenty of fibre to our diet. A single mango provides 40 per cent of our daily fibre requirement. Many of the tropical fruits contain powerful enzymes. These are chemicals that aid digestion and are particularly good at breaking down proteins such as cheese or meat. This is why pineapple has traditionally been served with gammon.

How are they eaten?

All tropical fruits can be eaten raw, either on their own or mixed with other ingredients – for example in a fruit salad or as a topping on meringue. They are great thirst quenchers and their strong flavours and bright colours makes them excellent for juices or smoothies.

Papayas may be served chilled as a starter with a squeeze of lime juice. Mangoes can also be cooked and served in dips, such as salsas, and chutneys. Many tropical fruits are preserved by canning and some are also available dried. However, they are much more nutritious if eaten fresh.

Choosing and storing tropical fruits

Choose undamaged fruit and allow it to ripen at room temperature. Never put bananas in the fridge or they will rot from the inside.

FOOD FACTS

Bananas are the world's most popular fruit. Many varieties are eaten raw but some, called plantains, must be cooked. The plantain is a staple food in many tropical countries, taking the role of the potato in cooler regions.

 Pineapples and bananas are part of many people's weekly shop. Air transport has made tropical fruits widely available in supermarkets around the world.

Pineapple and ham pizza

SERVES: 2 | **PREPARATION TIME: 40 MINUTES** | **COOKING TIME: 20–30 MINUTES**

Sometimes called a Hawaiian pizza, this combination of ham and pineapple makes a great pizza topping.

Ingredients
200g strong bread flour,
     plus extra for dusting
7g dried yeast
5g salt
125ml warm water
200g tin pineapple cubes
2 fresh tomatoes
50g Cheddar cheese
50g mozzarella cheese
50g cooked ham
1 tablespoon vegetable oil

1. Put the flour, yeast and salt into a bowl. Add the warm water and mix to form a soft dough.

2. Place the dough on a lightly floured work surface and knead (see page 47) for 10 minutes.

3. Preheat the oven to 200°C/ gas mark 6.

4. Stretch the dough into a circle and place it on a baking tray. Cover it with cling film and leave it to rise for 20 minutes.

5. In the meantime, drain the tin of pineapple cubes.

6. Cut the tomatoes into slices about 5mm thick. Grate all the cheese and tear the ham into bite-sized pieces.

7. Brush the pizza base with the oil and bake it on its own for 5 minutes.

8. When the base it ready, take it out of the oven and place the tomato slices on top of it. Then add the ham, cheese and pineapple cubes.

9. Bake for 20 minutes until the base is crispy and the topping is golden brown.

Banana and mango shake

SERVES: 2 | **PREPARATION TIME: 20 MINUTES** | **COOKING TIME: NO COOKING**

Tropical fruits work really well in smoothies and fruit juices. This drink combines two of the word's favourite fruits.

Ingredients
½ ripe mango
1 banana
150ml milk
120ml orange juice
2 teaspoons lime juice
1 tablespoon caster sugar
2 heaped teaspoons vanilla
   frozen yoghurt

1. Peel the mango and cut the flesh away from the stone. Dice the flesh.

2. Peel and dice the banana.

3. Put the mango and banana in a blender and add all the other ingredients. Whizz for about 30 seconds to make a light and frothy drink.

4. Pour the shake into tall glasses and serve immediately.

Far Eastern fruit salad

SERVES: 4 | **PREPARATION TIME: 15–20 MINUTES** | **COOKING TIME: NO COOKING**

You can use any tropical fruit in this salad. Try adding kiwi fruit instead of the grapes.

Ingredients
425g can lychees in syrup
3 pieces stem ginger plus
   2 tablespoons of the syrup
zest and juice of one lime
2 oranges, cut into
   small pieces
1 mango, peeled and diced
200g black or red grapes
1 banana

1. Drain the lychees over a bowl.

2. Discard half the syrup, then add the lychees to the bowl.

3. Add all the other ingredients and stir well.

4. Spoon into bowls and serve.

 COOK'S TIP

If you are not serving the salad straight away, do not add the bananas as they will go brown. Add them just before serving instead.

Glossary

antioxidant — a type of vitamin substance believed to protect body cells from damage and ageing

beta carotene — one of a group of yellow and red pigments contained in some plants

blanching — to precook something for a very short time

carbohydrate — a nutrient that gives the body energy

cereal — the grain that comes from edible grasses, such as rice and oats

chutney — a thick, spicy accompaniment to food, made of chopped fruits or vegetables cooked in vinegar and sugar with spices

coulis — a fruit purée thin enough to pour

crouton — a small, crisp piece of toasted or fried bread, usually eaten in soups or salads, such as Caesar salad

diabetes — a medical condition in which the body is unable to control the level of sugar in the blood

enzyme — a chemical agent that changes food into substances that our bodies can absorb

feta cheese — a firm Greek cheese with a tangy flavour made from sheep's milk

fibre — the bulky part of food, known as roughage, that is needed for digestion

iron — a mineral found in certain foods, such as green leafy vegetables, pulses and meat, which our body needs to be healthy

knead — to make dough soft and elastic by folding and pummelling

legume — the seed or pod of a plant of the pea or bean family

lycopene — a red pigment found in tomatoes and other foods, which works as an antioxidant in the body

magnesium — a mineral found in certain foods, such as green vegetables, which our body needs in order to be healthy

mineral — a substance, such as iron, that is found in the soil and the foods we eat

nutrient — any part of a food that gives the body energy or the goodness it needs to grow

par boiled — when something is boiled before roasting or frying

perishable — likely to rot or go bad quickly

pesticide — a chemical substance that is used to kill pests or weeds. Washing fruit and vegetables is important as it removes pesticides

preserve — to keep something in its existing state, for example, by eating fruit and vegetables raw, you preserve their vitamin and minerals

potassium — a mineral found in certain foods, such as squashes and bananas, which our body needs in order to be healthy

pulses — the seeds of pod-bearing plants such as beans, which can be dried and used as food

purée — food that has been cooked then mashed or blended until it makes a smooth, thick pulp

risotto — an Italian dish of rice cooked in stock with vegetables, meat or fish

salsa — a spicy sauce of chopped, usually uncooked vegetables such as onion, tomatoes, chilli and peppers

saturated fat — a type of fat that is harmful to the body because it builds up in the arteries and causes heart disease

staple — basic, necessary

sub-tropical — belonging to the area north and south of the Tropics; the climate is generally hot and humid in summer and mild or cool in winter

temperate — mild

toxin — a poisonous substance

vitamin — a special substance found in food, which the body needs in tiny amounts to stay healthy

Food safety

Each year there are about 70,000 food poisoning cases reported in the UK alone. Sticking to some simple rules can help you avoid this and other kitchen dangers.

1. Clean all your work surfaces before you start cooking.

2. If you have long hair, tie it back away from your face.

3. To avoid a serious injury, always wear shoes in the kitchen.

4. Wash your hands well with soap and warm water before you start to cook. Wash them after handling any raw meat, poultry or fish.

5. Read through the recipe you are cooking before you start. Check that you have all the equipment and ingredients that you will need.

6. Check the sell-by dates on all food.

7. Wash all fruit and vegetables under cold running water.

8. When preparing food, keep it out of the refrigerator for the shortest time possible. Generally, you should not leave food out of the fridge for more than 2 hours.

9. Use a different chopping board and knife to prepare meat, chicken and fish from the one you use for preparing fruit and vegetables.

10. Never serve under-cooked food, ensure that any meat, fish and chicken is cooked all the way through.

11. Replace used tea towels regularly with clean, dry ones to avoid the spreading of bacteria.

 KNOW YOUR FOOD

Useful information
These abbreviations have been used:
ml – millilitre   **g** – gram
cm – centimetre   **mm** – milimetre

1 teaspoon = 5 mililitres
1 tablespoon = 15 mililitres

All eggs are medium unless stated.

Cooking temperatures:
To work out where the cooker dial needs to be for high, medium and low heat, count the marks on the dial and divide them by three. The top few are high, the bottom few are low and the in-between ones are medium.

Useful techniques

Dicing
Cut the fruit or vegetable intro strips about 1 cm wide, then chop the vegetable to give you cubes about 1 cm in size.

Blanching
Place the vegetables in a saucepan with just enough boiling water to cover them. Keep them in the water for the required time, which will vary depending on the recipe.

Rubbing in
Use your fingertips to 'squash' the butter into the flour. Continue to do this until the flour resembles bread crumbs.

Mashing
Use either a fork or a masher to press down to squash the fruit or vegetable. Continue to do this until there are no lumps left.

Peeling tomatoes
Use a sharp knife to make a cross at the bottom of the tomato. Cover the tomato with boiling water and leave to stand for 3 minutes before removing. The skin should peel back from the cross.

Poaching eggs
Put water in a saucepan to boil. When it is boiling, stir it to create a 'whirlpool'. Crack the egg into the water and allow it to boil for the desired length of time.

Kneading
Press down on the dough with the palm of your hand, then fold the dough over itself and press down again. Continue to do this until the dough is soft and elastic.

Index

Useful websites

For information on ingredients and cookery techniques, log on to:

http://thefoody.com/basic/index.html or
http://www.bbc.co.uk/food/glossary/

For step-by-step video guides to cookery techniques, log on to:

http://www.waitrose.com/food/cookingandrecipes/cookinglibraries/
howtovideos.aspx

For recipes for every occasion as well as tips for planning menus, log on to

http://www.bbc.co.uk/food/recipes/

FOOD & HOW TO COOK IT!

Contents of titles in series:

EGGS AND DAIRY
978 0 7502 5662 9

Eggs, dairy foods and a balanced diet
Looking at eggs
Egg recipes
Looking at dairy foods
Milk
Milk recipes
Cheese
Cheese recipes
Butter and cream
Butter and cream recipes
Yoghurt
Yoghurt recipes
Food safety
Useful techniques

FRUIT AND VEGETABLES
978 0 7502 5659 9

Plants and a balanced diet
Looking at vegetables
Looking at fruits
Salad vegetables
Salad vegetable recipes
Roots and tubers
Roots and tuber recipes
Green vegetables
Green vegetable recipes
Vegetable fruits
Vegetable fruit recipes
Legumes and pulses
Legume and pulse recipes
Orchard fruits
Orchard fruit recipes
Berries and currants
Berry and currant recipes
Citrus fruits
Citrus fruit recipes
Tropical fruits
Tropical fruit recipes
Food safety
Useful techniques

GRAINS AND CEREALS
978 0 7502 5660 5

Cereals and a balanced diet
Farming and processing
Rice
Rice recipes
Wheat
Wheat recipes
Oats
Oats recipes
Maize
Maize recipes
Barley
Barley recipes
Rye
Rye recipes
Millet and sorghum
Millet and sorghum recipes
Food safety
Useful techniques

MEAT AND FISH
978 0 7502 5661 2

Meat, fish and a balanced diet
Looking at meat and poultry
Looking at fish
How to handle meat and fish
Beef
Beef recipes
Lamb
Lamb recipes
Pork
Pork recipes
Chicken and other poultry
Chicken recipes
Fish and shellfish
Fish and shellfish recipes
Food safety
Useful techniques